WHAT'S INSIDE!

Welcome to another totally inappropriate coloring book, the original cheekily profane (yet positive) adult coloring book series. Check out a few of the 25 fabulous designs in this book, just waiting for you to color them:

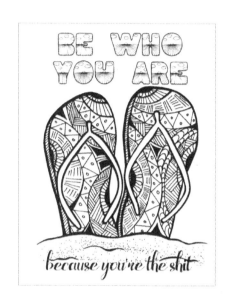

LET'S GET COLORING!

The Totally Inappropriate Coloring Books:

YOU'RE THE SHIT
YOU'RE TOTALLY BADASS
YOU ARE ONE BAMF
F♥CK CANCER*

*(a portion of the proceeds donated to research dedicated to finding a cure for cancer)

You're Totally Badass

A totally inappropriate self-affirming
ADULT COLORING BOOK

Designed by
JEN MEYERS

Please Note: This books contains adult language
and is not intended for children.

Published in August 2016 by Turning Leaves Press, Inc.

Artwork © Andriy Lipkan, Somjai Jaithieng, Irinakrivoruchko, Kulikoks, Olesia
Agudova, Vienybe, Frescomovie, Ekmelica, Pe3ak, Lexver :: www.dreamstime.com

ISBN 978-1546619635

WELCOME!

THIS is your lucky day! *You're Totally Badass* has even more sass and spunk than the original totally inappropriate self-affirming coloring book, *You're the Shit*, and you have it grasped in your serendipitous hands right now. Seriously, how much luckier could you get? (I'm just saying.) Because this book is filled with love, light, positivity...and a metric shit ton of shameless swearing.

What stresses you out? School? Work? Family? Life in general? Whatever it is, coloring lets you escape to a vibrant world of your own making.

Coloring is such a fantastic way to relax and unwind, to unfocus from the problems of the world, and bring a world of calming color into your own. And we can all use some more calm (and color, for that matter) in our lives, now can't we?

My sincere hope is that this book makes you smile and laugh as you color your way through the gorgeous designs. As you do, I hope you know that you are...

❖ a complete and utter badass,

❖ totally the shit,

❖ and fucking awesome

...just because you're YOU.

Now grab your pencils or gel pens, find a nice quiet place, and color the shit out of this book. Happy coloring!

Inappropriately yours,
JEN

P.S. If you like this book, there are more Totally Inappropriate coloring books available: *You're the Shit, You are One BAMF,* and *F*ck Cancer* (a portion of the proceeds from the cancer coloring book is being donated to support research dedicated to finding a cure for cancer. Because fuck cancer.)

You are

the shitest

YOU ARE
INFUCKINGCREDIBLE

Be your own fucking fairy godmother

you are MY fucking cup of tea
just the way you are

I love the shit out of you

Do the things that fucking exhilarate you

Each day counts

so enjoy every fucking cupcake

Nothing more sweetss

than You

I just fucking

love you
that is all

Embrace your

BADASSERY

Thank You!

I think you are a total badass for picking up this book, and I truly hope you enjoyed it. If you did, would you be so kind as to post a review wherever you purchased it? And please don't be a stranger! Drop me a line at jen@jmeyersbooks.com or visit me on Facebook at www.facebook.com/jmeyersbooks. I'm also on Twitter and Instagram as @jmeyersbooks.

Hope to meet you soon!
JEN

JEN MEYERS grew up in Vermont, spent three years in Germany when she was a kid, and now lives in central New York. When she's not reading, writing, or designing coloring books, she's chasing after her four kids, playing outside, relishing the few quiet moments she gets with her husband, and forgetting to make dinner.

Besides designing Totally Inappropriate coloring books, she also writes contemporary romance and young adult fantasy. She is the author of the (completely appropriate) *Intangible* series, the (perfectly inappropriate) *Happily Ever After* series and *Anywhere*, and co-author of the (totally inappropriate) *Untamed* series. For more information about Jen and her work, visit her website www.jmeyersbooks.com.

Made in the USA
Las Vegas, NV
17 December 2021

38372498R00033